PETE AND PENNY
PLAY AND PRAY

D1525004

PETE AND PENNY
PLAY AND PRAY

Devotional Readings for Boys and Girls
Five to Nine Years Old

by

DOROTHY GRUNBOCK JOHNSTON

MOODY PRESS • CHICAGO

Printed in the United States of America

Contents

Introduction

Pete and Penny Play and Pray is the first volume in a series designed for use by boys and girls who have reached that point in life where the habit of personal devotions should be developed. This habit starts with family devotions or, in all likelihood, does not start at all. When the family as a unit follows a specific plan of daily devotions, the child will be encouraged to do so also on his own.

This book may be read in family devotions by a parent or by the child himself. It may be given to the child as his very own devotional reading; however, he may be apt to read it right through as one story. It should be read one chapter at a time, daily or alternated with Bible readings or on a certain day of the week.

The Bible is the foundation and center of family devotions, but other books based upon the Bible should be used to clarify Bible teachings for young children. The Pete and Penny series is planned for that purpose. Each chapter is an episode in a continuous story and has a threefold objective: (1) to tell a story, (2) to present a Bible truth or instruction, and (3) to provide the actual scripture verses bearing upon that truth—all put together in an entertaining form.

The author has a large family of her own, and what she has set forth in these pages are the ideas and instructions she has found most effective and satisfactory.

Off for a Vacation

PETE AND PENNY PENDLETON, who lived with their father and mother in Seattle, went to the beach along Puget Sound in the state of Washington, for a two-week vacation. Puget Sound is a large body of water like a huge bay stretching inland from the sea. The family of four camped on the beach. How the twins loved to camp out, especially when they could sleep right on the beach, far up from the water's edge!

One day Pete and Penny were walking along on the beach with their daddy. Pete looked up with big brown eyes. "Who is God?" he asked.

Daddy sat on a log and motioned for Pete and Penny to sit beside him.

"Who is God?" repeated Daddy. "Why, the great Lord God is the Creator of the whole wide world."

"*Creator*," chimed in Penny, "means God made everything."

Daddy always carried a little Bible in his pocket. The print was tiny, but he could read it. He turned to the Thirty-third Psalm.

Pete tossed a stone into the water and listened to it splash. Then he listened while Daddy read:

The earth is full of the goodness of the LORD. By the word of the LORD were the heavens made; and all the host of them by the breath of his mouth . . . Let all the earth fear the LORD: let all the inhabitants of the world stand in awe of him. For he spake, and it was done (Psalm 33:5-6, 8-9).

Penny didn't like to hear a big word she couldn't understand.

"What does *inhabitant* mean, Daddy?"

"An inhabitant is a person who lives in this world that God has made. You and Pete and I are inhabitants because we live on the earth. We read, 'Let all the inhabitants of the world stand in awe of him.' *You* could say, 'Let the world be made'; and nothing would happen. But when *God* spoke, it was done. When the Bible says, 'stand in awe of Him,' it means, 'just think how wonderful God is to be able to do that.' "

Pete and Penny listened while Daddy told them, "A long time ago there was no earth, no sun, no moon, no stars. There were no flowers or animals or people. There was nothing. Then God spoke and all these things were made."

Pete wrinkled up his forehead. "But where did God come from, Daddy?"

"God always was," replied Daddy. "There never

11

was a time when God wasn't." Then he read from another psalm in the Bible:

> Before the mountains were brought forth, or ever thou hadst formed the earth and the world, even from everlasting to everlasting, thou art God (Psalm 90:2).

"Let's thank Him," said Penny. "Let's thank God for the wonderful world He made."

So that is what Pete and Penny and Daddy did, sitting there on the log.

Sleeping Under the Stars

PETE PUFFED and snorted and puffed some more. He was trying to blow air into his rubber air mattress so he could sleep on it. Penny already had put the plug in hers and was unrolling her sleeping bag on top of it.

Tonight, Pete and Penny and Daddy and Mommy were going to sleep right on the beach beside the water, out under the stars. Soon each one had crawled into his sleeping bag and had zipped it up.

It was fun to lie there and look.

At first, after the flashlights were turned off, the world looked dark and black. But Pete saw a star twinkle in the sky. Then he saw another and another.

12

The more he looked, the more he saw. Why, the whole sky was blinking with a thousand eyes—and they were all stars.

Daddy knew lots of Bible verses by heart. When he saw the stars, it made him want to say one, so he did:

> The heavens declare the glory of God; and the firmament showeth his handiwork (Psalm 19:1).

"Too many big words," said Penny. "What do they all mean?"

"*Declare* means to tell," said Daddy. "The heavens tell us something. They tell us about the glory of God."

"Glory? Please explain," Penny's voice said in the darkness.

"God is great and wonderful," answered Daddy. "He is the only One who could make the stars, and He is the only One who could make them stay in the sky and not fall down."

"Stars aren't really tiny like they look, are they, Daddy?" It was Pete's voice.

"Stars are really very, very large. They are millions of miles away. That is why they look so tiny."

Mommy's voice was heard. "Stars aren't the only things in the heaven that declare the glory of God. The sun is a big ball of fire, yet God keeps it just the right distance from the earth so that we are nice and warm. If the sun were closer, we would burn up. If the sun were farther away, we would freeze. I'm glad God made the sun. I'm glad He keeps it in the right place. It tells me of His glory."

Just then, Pete got up on his elbow. He looked toward the east and then he whistled. Behind the jagged black outline that the fir trees made against the sky, the moon was slowly rising. It was a big full moon, as round and orange as a pumpkin.

Penny saw it too. "The heavens do declare the glory of God, don't they? The moon is in the heavens and it tells me how great God is."

"Yes, 'the heavens declare the glory of God;' " said Daddy, " 'and the firmament showeth his handiwork' (Psalm 19:1)."

"Explain the rest, please," asked Penny.

"Tomorrow," promised Daddy. "Let's pray now. Let's thank God for the sun and moon and stars that tell us of His glory."

So they did.

Out of the Sleeping Bags

PENNY WAS THE FIRST to wake up, and she remembered Daddy's promise. When she saw him wiggle his nose, she knew he was awake.

"Explain it now," she said. " 'The heavens declare the glory of God and the firmament showeth His handiwork.' Explain the last part."

"Well," said Daddy, "your handiwork is something you make. It is work that you make with your hands."

Pete was pretending to be asleep, but he was listening. Now he sat up. "I whittled a boat from a piece of wood yesterday," he said. "Was that handiwork?"

"Yes," said Daddy. Then he went on. *"Firmament* means the heaven or the skies above. The clouds, the sun, moon, and stars are *God's* handiwork."

> For by him were all things created, that are in heaven, and that are in the earth, . . . all things were created by him, and for him (Colossians 1:16).

Penny jumped out of her sleeping bag and was ready to start the day, for she had gone to sleep with her clothes on. That is the way campers do, sometimes. Of course she took time to comb her brown

curly hair, which was the color of chestnuts, and push a wave into her bangs.

She saw a daisy on the bank beyond the beach. She picked it. "This flower is God's handiwork, too," she said. She looked at the yellow center. It was as though a hundred tiny yellow pinheads had been set into a perfect pattern. The long white petals stuck out gracefully, but they were fastened tightly to the green cap that held the stem.

"Why," said Penny, "if I tried and tried, I could never make a flower."

"There are plastic flowers in the dime store," Pete said. "Some of them look real, too."

"But this flower *grew,*" said Penny. "It is alive. And it smells good, too. Its petals are soft and smooth. Why, a flower is beautiful. It is God's handiwork."

Mommy was stirring pancake batter. "Think how many kinds of flowers there are," she suggested. "There are red roses, white lilies, pansies that look like faces, red poppies, tiny violets, and big sunflowers. Each one has its own color and shape and smell. They are all wonderful; and God made them, every one."

And God said, Let the earth bring forth grass, . . . and the fruit tree yielding fruit after his kind, whose seed is in itself, upon the earth: and it was so (Genesis 1:11).

17

"When God made each plant, He made it so it would grow and make more plants just like the first one," Mommy continued. " 'He hath made every thing beautiful' (Ecclesiastes 3:11). Let's thank Him for the beautiful flowers."

Penny Lands a Fish

AFTER BREAKFAST, Pete and Penny and Daddy got into the rowboat and went fishing. Daddy rowed. Penny put a wriggling worm on her hook and turned the little crank on her reel. The line went out behind the boat. Pete was just starting to let his line out when Penny squealed.

"It jerked. It's jerking again. A fish. I have a fish!"

"Reel in! Reel in!" shouted Daddy.

Penny turned her reel and wound up the line. The fish kept jumping and twisting and splashing, but Penny kept cranking.

Pretty soon the fish was beside the boat. Daddy held a net under so that it wouldn't fall off the hook and be lost. And soon the fish was flopping in the boat.

"It's a beauty," Pete called out. "Dad, it sure is a beauty."

"My first trout," said Penny happily.

"Trout are delicious," explained Pete. "Eat it for lunch, Penny."

"It really is pretty. See the black speckles." Penny was delighted.

"God made fish," reminded Daddy.

> God said, Let the waters bring forth abundantly the moving creature that hath life, and fowl that may fly above the earth in the open firmament of heaven. And God created great whales, and every living creature that moveth, which the waters brought forth abundantly, after their kind, and every winged fowl after his kind: and God saw that it was good (Genesis 1: 20-21).

Just then a sea gull screeched overhead. Penny looked up. She loved to watch a sea gull, its feet tucked close to its body, glide gracefully through the air.

"I wish I could fly like a bird," she said.

"God is very great and wise to be able to make a bird," said Daddy. "We can praise His name this minute. We can thank God that He is so great and so wise."

A Tiny Visitor

PENNY SAT on a big rock on the beach and ate her trout for lunch. Mommy had fried it crisp and brown over the campfire. She shared it with Pete, because he hadn't caught one.

Just as she started to take another bite, a chipmunk whisked his tail in a tree above and scolded. In a loud, high voice he said, "Che-che-che-che!" as fast as a fire engine's wheels go around.

Penny tossed a piece of bread toward the bank which rose up from the beach farther back; and when the little fellow finally sneaked close enough to snatch it, Penny could see his shiny brown eyes and the two tan stripes that ran down his brown back.

"He is a pretty little animal," she said. "He is one of God's creatures. God made him, and God takes care of him."

"You are right," agreed Daddy. Then he quoted a Bible verse.

> And God said, Let the earth bring forth the living creature after his kind, cattle, and creeping thing, and beast of the earth after his kind: and it was so (Genesis 1:24).

"What does 'after his kind' mean?" asked Penny.

"God created the first little chipmunks," said Daddy, "and He made them so that a mamma and a daddy chipmunk can have baby chipmunks. A mother mouse and a father mouse have baby mice. The chipmunk babies look like their chipmunk parents, and live and eat as they do. The mice babies look like mice parents. A mother and a father skunk have baby skunks, and their babies look like their skunk parents and eat the same things."

"And smell the same," Pete piped up.

Daddy laughed. "Yes, and smell the same. That's what 'after his kind' means. Each creature, whether it is a rabbit or a creeping thing like a snake, or a beast like a lion, has babies of its own kind."

Mommy had been munching peanuts for dessert. Now she reached into Daddy's pocket and took out his little Bible. She knew where to find verses that told about God's creatures.

> There be four things which are little upon the earth, but they are exceeding wise: The ants are a people not strong, yet they prepare their meat in the summer; The conies are but a feeble folk, yet make their houses in the rocks; The locusts have no king, yet go they forth all of them by bands; The spider taketh hold with her hands, and is in kings' palaces (Proverbs 30:24-28).

Mommy smiled at Pete and Penny. "God made every animal, every insect, every creature you can think of; and He gave each one the know-how to take care of itself and to find food."

An Old Man with a Sack

PETE AND PENNY were wondering, later that afternoon, what to do for excitement, when they heard a crunching sound on the stones.

They had not seen anyone else on the beach or in the woods, so they were surprised to see an old man trudging along the beach, coming toward them.

On his back he carried a gunnysack. Something heavy was in that sack, because the old man was bent low.

When he looked up, they saw that his face was very brown and wrinkled. He was an Indian.

Daddy said hello and then politely asked what made the sack so heavy.

The Indian said, "Clams."

Daddy asked if he could buy some, and the old man said yes. Then he would not have so many to carry.

Pete and Penny could hardly wait until supper.

They carefully washed the sand off the outside of each clam. They put them all into a pan, and Pete covered them with fresh water. Penny put the lid on the pan and set it on the grate.

Pete poked the fire. Then he got more wood from along the beach where the tide had left it.

"We should have dug our own clams," Pete said.

"The old Indian probably needed the money," Penny replied. "We can dig some another day."

The children both loved to cook, and clams were easy. All they had to do now, was to wait until the water boiled. After the clams boiled a few minutes, they would open by themselves. Then they would be ready to eat.

While they waited, Penny set the picnic table and Pete peeled peaches. Mother made the salad and got the rest of the supper ready.

After a while, Penny peeked into the pan. The water was bubbling and boiling. Soon it was time to lift the open clams out onto a plate and serve them.

While they ate, Pete thought of something.

"Daddy," he said, "God made the wide world and everything in it, and He knows all about everything that goes on. But *why* did God make the world?"

"God made the world for people to live in," said Daddy, "and God made people to be His friends.

24

God the Father and God the Son, who is Jesus, have always been in heaven. They were there long before the world was ever made. The Bible tells us that they were rejoicing, which means They were happy about something."

"What were They happy about?" Penny inquired.

"They were happy about the *habitable* part of the earth. That means the parts of the earth where people would live. They were happy that there were going to be people who would love Them and believe in Them and be Their friends."

Daddy had been fingering through the pages of his Bible. Pete and Penny and Mother listened while he said, "This is God the Son talking." Then he read:

> The Lord possessed me in the beginning of his way, before his works of old. I was set up from everlasting, from the beginning, or ever the earth was. . . . . I was . . . with him: and I was daily his delight, rejoicing always before him; rejoicing in the habitable part of his earth; and my delights were with the sons of men (Proverbs 8:22-23; 30-31).

A Boat Ride at Night

JUST BEFORE it was time to crawl into their sleeping bags, Daddy took Pete and Penny and Mother for a short ride in the rowboat.

The night was black. There were no stars peeping down, and the moon was not shining.

Pete was in the bow of the boat, right up in the very front. The ripples that flowed away from the boat on each side sparkled.

Pete looked over the edge of the boat. "I see fish," he said in a hoarse whisper. "Look! Lots of fish."

The fish, startled by the big boat, swam away in all directions and left streaks of light trailing behind them in the water.

Penny dabbled her fingers in the water. The drops that dripped from her fingers sparkled like a million diamonds.

"What is this, Daddy? What makes the water full of tiny lights?"

"That is phosphorus," explained Daddy. "Tiny, wee animals are in the water, and they have something in their bodies that gleams and glows. I am glad that it is really dark. We can see the phosphorus better."

When Daddy splashed with his oars, the water fell

in pools of light. It was fun to stir the water which was full of phosphorus, and see it shine.

"The bright sparkle makes me think of a Christmas tree with a million lights," said Pete.

Daddy was ready with a question. "Why do we celebrate Christmas?"

"Why?" repeated Pete. "Because it's Jesus' birthday."

"Jesus was born a little baby like I was, wasn't He, Daddy?" inquired Penny.

"Before the world was made, God the Son was in heaven with God the Father. When Adam and Eve sinned and God knew that everyone else would sin too, He promised to send His Son from heaven to take your punishment and mine, and make it possible for us to be right with God."

Mother added, "Lots of people didn't believe God would keep His promise. They got tired of waiting and watching for Jesus."

"Finally," said Daddy, "the right day came. And Jesus, who had been with God in heaven, became a little baby and was born into this world, just as you were, Penny."

"There was one big difference," said Mother. "You have a human mother and a human father. Jesus'

28

mother was a sweet young woman named Mary, but God in heaven was His Father."

"It was a happy day when Jesus was born," said Penny. "I know, because angels came and told some shepherds. I know those Bible verses by heart."

And there were in the same country shepherds abiding in the field, keeping watch over their flock by night. And, lo, the angel of the Lord came upon them, and the glory of the Lord shone round about them: and they were sore afraid. And the angel said unto them, Fear not: for, behold, I bring you good tidings of great joy, which shall be to all people. For unto you is born this day in the city of David a Saviour, which is Christ the Lord. And this shall be a sign unto you; Ye shall find the babe wrapped in swaddling clothes, lying in a manger. And suddenly there was with the angel a multitude of the heavenly host praising God, and saying, Glory to God in the highest, and on earth peace, good will toward men (Luke 2: 8-14).

Later, when Penny closed her eyes in her sleeping bag, she was still thinking about the sweet baby Jesus.

A Whistle from the Willow

PETE AND PENNY decided to climb up into a big madrona tree. Its bark was a bright reddish-brown color, and it was fun to peel off the old layers that were drying up. Underneath, the new bark was soft and smooth as satin.

Pete leaned back in the crotch of the tree and took out his pocketknife.

"I think I'll carve my initials," he said.

Penny watched him make the first *P*.

"We really should call you Pep, because your name is Peter Edward Pendleton, and your initials are P.E.P."

"Well, then we should call you Pep, too, because your name is Penelope Elaine Pendleton, and your initials are P.E.P.—the same as mine."

Penny laughed. "Then when Mother would say, 'Pep, please set the table,' we'd both rush to do it."

"We'd better let everybody keep on calling us Pete and Penny like they have been." Pete started to make an *E*.

Daddy came and stood below. "Having fun?" he asked.

"Sure," answered Pete. "This is the best vacation we ever had."

When the children climbed down, Daddy asked if he could borrow Pete's knife. They watched Daddy whittle on a willow branch he had in his hand. They knew he was going to make a whistle for each of them.

"Once," said Daddy, "there was a tree that was very important to you and me."

"What tree was that?" asked Pete.

"It was the tree on which they hung Jesus," replied Daddy. "The Bible says, 'Christ . . . suffered for us, . . . who did no sin, . . . who his own self bare our sins in his own body on the tree' (1 Peter 2:2-24)."

"I thought they hung Him on a cross," said Penny.

"The cross was a wood cross made from a tree," said Daddy.

"If Jesus was God's Son and never sinned or did wrong things, why did they kill Him?" Penny asked.

Daddy quoted another verse in his Bible.

> For Christ also hath once suffered for sins, the just for the unjust, that he might bring us to God (1 Peter 3:18).

Then while Daddy whittled, he explained, "Jesus was *just,* that means He was good and never sinned. You and I are *unjust.* We have done wrong things. We have sinned. Jesus suffered and died for us for one reason."

"Why?" asked Pete.

"I told you why," Daddy replied. "It was 'that he might bring us to God.' "

"Now God must be happy," said Penny. "Jesus died so He could bring us to God. Now we are God's friends, and that is what God wanted in the first place. He wants people to be His friends."

"Some people are God's friends; some people aren't," answered Daddy. "I want to be sure I am His friend. Do you want to make sure that you are?"

Toot, Toot, Toot

PETE AND PENNY watched Daddy cut around the piece of willow branch he held in his hand. They watched him slip the moist bark off the slippery wood and notch the stick. Then they watched as he pushed the bark back on the stick. They listened while he blew on one end. It made a long, high note.

Daddy had made a whistle that worked.

He handed it to Penny. She made it go "Toot, toot, toot."

"Make me one, please," coaxed Pete.

He knew Daddy already had started to make one for him, but he asked for the whistle anyway.

While Daddy worked on a whistle for Pete, Penny puckered up her forehead.

"I want to be God's friend," she said. "I want to be *sure* I am God's friend and He is my Friend. I try to be good, Daddy, so God will be happy about me."

"No matter how hard you try to be good, Penny," said Daddy, "you can't be good enough." He stopped whittling, opened his Bible, and read a couple of verses.

> There is none that doeth good, no, not one. For all have sinned, and come short of the glory of God (Romans 3:12, 23).

"If it doesn't help to be good, then what is the use to try?" Penny pouted.

"If you want to be God's friend, you will have to do things God's way; because He is the One who is great and good and wise. Jesus, God's Son, said, 'Ye are my friends, if ye do whatsoever I command you' (John 15:14). One thing He commanded was this: He said, 'ye must be born again' " (John 3:7).

"I was born one time," said Penny. "I was a tiny baby and I was born into our family. Now I am a big girl. How can I be born again?"

"You were born into the Pendleton family," said Daddy. He slipped his arm around Penny and gave her a little squeeze. "But you also need to be born into God's family."

"I don't know how," sobbed Penny. She hid her face in her hands, and her brown curls tumbled over her hands.

"Listen while I say John 3:16 for you. It will tell you how to be born into God's family."

> For God so loved the world, that he gave his only begotten Son, that whosoever believeth in him should not perish, but have everlasting life (John 3:16).

"You need to be a 'whosoever,' " said Daddy. "You must believe in your heart that Jesus died for *you,* Penny."

"He died for everybody," Penny said. "Not for just me."

"True, He died for the whole world, but everyone in the world isn't God's friend. Everyone doesn't have everlasting life. Everyone isn't born again. I am, Penny. Do you want to believe that the Lord Jesus Christ died for *you?*"

Penny did not answer. She wanted to think.

Penny Goes for a Boat Ride

PETE AND PENNY each had a whistle now. They thanked Daddy and ran toward the beach to play.

"Mother, Mother," called Penny. "Mother, may I please go for a ride in the rowboat?"

"Not unless Daddy goes with you," said Mother. "You know you are never, never to go out in the rowboat alone."

Penny ran back toward Daddy. "Take me rowing, Daddy, please," she pleaded.

"Not yet," said Daddy. "Mother and I are going back into the woods to pick berries. You and Pete play on the beach. I'll take you when I get back. Do as I say. If you disobey, I will have to punish you."

Penny watched Daddy and Mother disappear into the woods.

"I want to go out in the rowboat *now*." She pouted. "I don't want to wait an hour or two. I want to go now." Then she made up her mind. "I will go now," she said. "I won't stay long, and they won't know. You won't tell on me, will you, Pete?"

"Don't go, Penny," Pete warned. "Don't disobey Daddy. Don't go rowing by yourself."

"I'm going," declared Penny, as she lifted the anchor into the boat. "And don't you dare tell on me!" She tossed her head back and felt the brown curls tickle her neck.

Penny shoved the boat out; and as she did, she jumped in. She sat down and began to row. She knew how to row, because Daddy had taught her. It was fun to reach the oars far back and pull hard. Every time she pulled, the boat moved through the water. Penny rowed and rowed. Then she decided it was time to go back. So she pulled on just one oar until the boat turned around. Then she rowed back.

Penny pointed the bow toward the beach; and when she heard the bottom of the boat scrape on the sand, she pulled the oars in and jumped out.

"That was fun," she said to Pete. "Be sure you don't tell on me."

But Pete didn't need to tell. Mother and Daddy had gone on the path that loops back onto the beach, and they had seen Penny in the boat alone.

"I will have to punish you," said Daddy. "You disobeyed, and you must be punished."

Penny began to cry; but even though she was a big girl, Daddy pulled her across his knees. He raised his right hand, ready for the first hard whack.

"Please," pleaded Penny, "don't spank me. Don't!" She kicked her legs and squirmed.

Daddy went right ahead. The palm of his big hand hit hard one, two, three times.

37

Then Daddy set Penny onto her feet; and she stood there with her back to Daddy and Mother and Pete, sniffling.

"I'm sorry," said Daddy, "that I had to spank you, Penny; but I had to keep my word. I promised to punish you if you disobeyed me. You chose to disobey, so there was nothing for me to do but to punish you."

Penny nodded. She knew Daddy had done right, but she still did not like the feeling Daddy's big hand had made.

"It is hard to imagine," Daddy went on, "that Pete would ever offer to take the punishment you deserve." He winked at Pete, and Pete grinned. "But just suppose," said Daddy, "that Pete had offered to let me spank him for your disobedience."

"Then I would have gotten out of a spanking." Penny's face brightened.

"You are right," Daddy said. "I could spank only one person for that one act of disobedience. If Pete had offered to take the punishment you deserved, I could not have spanked you. Jesus took the punishment you deserve for all your sin. Remember this verse?"

> For Christ also hath once suffered for sins, the just for the unjust, that he might bring us to God (1 Peter 3:18).

Penny Believes John 3:16

PETE AND PENNY found a clay bank near a stream that ran on to the beach near their camp.

It was fun to get gobs of the gooey cool clay and squeeze it and pat it and mold it.

Pete made a round ball. Then he pushed it in here, pulled it out there, and pinched it another place.

"It is a dog's head," exclaimed Penny. "Pete, you know how to make a good dog."

Pete smiled. He kept on molding until his dog was done. Then he took another gob and started to shape another animal.

Penny shaped a little basket. Then she made a tiny baby and put him in the basket. She shaped tall weeds to put around it.

"Baby Moses in the bulrushes," she said.

"Let's go show Mother and Daddy," said Pete.

Mother and Daddy were surprised. They liked the clay things the children had made.

"Have you more clay?" asked Daddy. "I'd like to try to make something."

Pete gave Daddy a lump of clay, and Daddy began to mold it with his long, strong fingers.

Penny watched with round brown eyes. "It is a cross, Daddy. You made a cross."

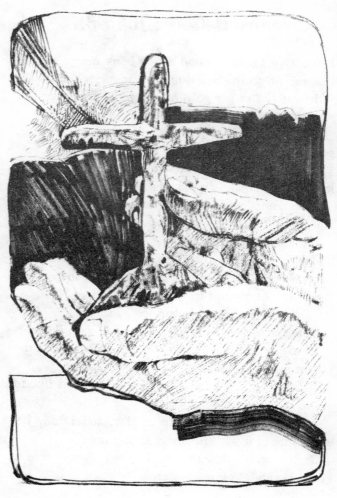

"I made a cross to remind you that the Lord Jesus Christ, God's only Son, died on a cross for you, Penny."

Penny did not ask, "Why did Jesus have to die for me?" because Penny knew why Jesus had had to die. She almost knew by heart the verse she had heard so often.

> For Christ also hath once suffered for sins, the just for the unjust, that he might bring us to God (1 Peter 3:18).

"The 'unjust' means me," Penny said out loud. "I have done wrong things. God calls the wrong things I do, sin."

"What wrong thing did you do lately?" asked Daddy.

Penny looked down at her bare toes. "I disobeyed," she answered. "I went in the rowboat alone when you told me not to."

Daddy nodded.

"I have disobeyed lots of other times," said Penny, "and I have told lies too, and—" Penny began to cry.

"Right this minute," began Daddy, "do you want to believe that the Lord Jesus Christ took the punishment that *you* deserve for every one of your sins?"

41

"Yes," answered Penny. "Right this minute, I believe."

Then they all bowed their heads; and Penny prayed, "Dear God, I disobeyed this morning. I've done lots of wrong things. I'm sorry. Thank You for sending the Lord Jesus Christ to take the punishment for all my sin. Thank You that He died on the cross for *me*. In Jesus' name. Amen."

Penny smiled through her tears.

"Now," said Daddy, "you can say John 3:16 like this: For God so loved Penny, that He gave His only begotten Son, that because Penny believes on Him, she shall not perish, but has everlasting life."

Penny Has New Life

PETE DECIDED TO PLAY on the tide flats while the tide was out. He liked to poke around at the water's edge.

Penny had another plan. She had seen wild rose bushes above the bank. Bright red seed pods, that looked like shiny red berries, were growing where pretty pink wild roses had grown before. Penny picked a panful of the red pods. Then she asked Mother for a big needle and a long piece of string.

Penny sat on the sand and strung her red beadlike berries into a pretty necklace.

After a while Pete came running up the beach, dangling a starfish.

It was bright orange and bumpy on one side. The underneath side of its five sprawling legs were covered with tiny feelers.

"Take it back to the water's edge," Penny told him. "It will die up here on the dry beach."

Mother and Daddy had come to see the starfish, too.

"Does everything that is alive, die sometime?" Penny asked.

"Everything," said Daddy. "Flowers are pretty when you pick them, but they get brown and die. Little birds die, and dogs die, and people die. You can't think of anything that is alive that won't die."

"I don't want to die." Penny shivered. "I like to be alive."

"We are still young." Pete comforted her. "We don't need to worry about dying for a long time."

"That is where you are wrong," Mother told Pete. "Everyone in the world doesn't grow up to be a grandma or a grandpa before dying. Tiny babies die, and little boys die, and big boys die, and young men die. No one knows how long he will live."

43

"That's why we need to be ready to die," added Daddy.

"What do you do to be ready?" asked Penny.

"If you are born again, you are ready," said Mother. "If you believe in your heart that Jesus died for you, you have everlasting life. The Bible says, 'He that believeth on the Son hath everlasting life: and he that believeth not the Son shall not see life; but the wrath of God abideth on him' (John 3:36)."

"I am ready," said Penny. "I believe that Jesus died for me to take the punishment I deserve for all my sin."

"Someday your body will die, Penny," explained Daddy. "You won't be able to open your eyes. You won't be able to walk. Your body will be dead. But the real you that lives inside your body won't be dead. The minute you die, your soul will go to be with God in heaven. You will be absent from the body but present with the Lord (2 Corinthians 5:8). And you will live with God in heaven forever and ever and ever. That is what everlasting life is."

"If our tiger cat dies, will he go to heaven?" asked Pete.

"No," answered Daddy, "animals don't have souls, but people do. Only people can have everlasting life, and only the people who do what Jesus said, can have it. Jesus said, 'verily, verily, I say unto you, He that believeth on me hath everlasting life' (John 6:47)."

"I believe," said Penny happily.

A House in a Tree

PETE AND PENNY built a tree house. A big madrona tree stood on the edge of the bank. Its thick branches grew straight toward the water, and its shiny green leaves drooped down toward the beach. The branches were a perfect place for a platform.

By scouting along the beach in both directions, the children found boards of all shapes and sizes. Like busy beavers, they worked all day, building a house in the madrona tree.

Penny found an orange crate. That made a good cupboard. She gathered sea shells, bleached white in the sun, and put them in a neat row for her dishes. Pete made a bench where they could sit and watch sea gulls and kingfishers.

"I wonder if we may sleep up here?" questioned Penny. "Wouldn't that be fun?"

The tree house was right by the camp where Mother and Daddy slept. They gave Pete and Penny permission to sleep in the tree house, which was really

45

just a platform. The shiny green madrona leaves and branches above were the roof.

The children carried their air mattresses up on the bank. Then it was easy to walk right out onto their house. The sleeping bags were heavy. Pete helped Penny carry hers. Then Penny helped Pete carry his.

"It's getting dark," puffed Pete. "The sun is almost down."

"I wonder if the moon will shine," said Penny. "How can we see?"

"We'll just have to go to bed," said Pete. "I want to go to bed early, anyway. It will be fun to sleep in our tree house."

Before they crawled in, Daddy read, by the light from the fire, about heaven.

> And there shall be no night there; and they need no candle, neither light of the sun; for the Lord God giveth them light (Revelation 22:5). And the twelve gates were twelve pearls; every several gate was of one pearl; and the street of the city was pure gold, as it were transparent glass . . . And the city had no need of the sun, neither of the moon, to shine in it: for the glory of God did lighten it, and the Lamb is the light thereof (Revelation 21:21, 23).

"'The Lamb,'" explained Mother, "is another name for Jesus. In heaven we won't need the sun or

46

moon or candles or any kind of light, because the glory of God and His Son, the Lord Jesus Christ, will be all the light we need."

When Penny snuggled down into her sleeping bag up in the tree house, she was happy. "I am so glad," she said to herself, "that Jesus is my Saviour and my Friend now. I belong to His family. And when I die I can live with Jesus forever in heaven."

Visitors Come to the Tree House

PETE AND PENNY played in the tree house all morning.

Pete made a rope ladder so that they could climb from the beach right into the tree house without climbing up onto the bank.

Penny rolled up the sleeping bags and put them along the edge against the bank for a couch. Then she broke off a branch from a fir tree and used it for a broom. Madrona trees lose their leaves all summer long. When the shiny green leaves turn brown, they come floating down. They crackle when they are stepped on.

"Such a mess!" said Penny, as she swept with her fir tree broom.

"Flowers," she said, when the sweeping was done. "We need flowers."

She ran up the bank and through the woods to an opening where wild sweet peas grew as thick as weeds. Soon she came back with a fistful of the rose-colored flowers. It was easy to find a tin can on the beach. She put the flowers in it.

"Time for our morning snack," she said.

Mother gave her a cantaloupe and a bunch of green grapes.

Penny cut the cantaloupe and scooped out the seeds. Then she cut thin slices and put them in big clamshells.

Just as Pete climbed the ladder, Mother and Daddy came to call. They stood on the bank and knocked on the tree trunk, because there was no door to knock on.

"Callers. How nice," said Penny. "Come right in."

The "company" sat on the sleeping-bag couch, and Pete and Penny sat on the bench.

Penny passed the clamshells. They all enjoyed eating the cantaloupe, sliced like wedges of water-melon.

"I am so glad that you prepared a party for us," said Daddy, helping himself to another slice. "You have a nice place here. I know of another nice place

49

that is being prepared for everyone who is God's friend."

Daddy took out his Bible. "Jesus' friends were sad," he said, "when He told them He would leave them. Then Jesus told them about heaven."

> Let not your heart be troubled: ye believe in God, believe also in me. In my Father's house are many mansions: if it were not so, I would have told you. I go to prepare a place for you. And if I go and prepare a place for you, I will come again, and receive you unto myself; that where I am, there ye may be also (John 14:1-3).

"The Lord Jesus," said Mother, "has promised to prepare a place for us because we believe in Him. He is our Saviour."

"I am glad," said Penny, "that I am saved. I was saved the day I believed that Jesus died for me. That means I will get to live in a place that Jesus has prepared for me—when I go to be with Him."

A Swing over the Water

"PETE," SAID DADDY, "I have been looking at that big maple tree leaning out from the bank.

"All the trees on the bank lean over toward the

water," answered Pete. "I guess they are reaching for the light."

"That maple tree wouldn't be too hard to climb," said Daddy, "and there is a long, thick rope in the car trunk."

"A swing?" Pete asked. "Do you mean we can have a swing?" His brown eyes twinkled.

That was what Daddy meant. Soon Pete was high in the maple tree, tying the rope in a strong knot, as Daddy had shown him. Carefully he came down the tree. Daddy had tied a loop in the other end of the long rope, for a seat.

Pete wanted to be the first one to stand on the bank and then swing out over the beach. But he remembered the Bible verse, "Love one another." If he'd just tell Penny he loved her, she wouldn't believe it, unless he'd act like it sometimes.

So Pete said, "Here, Penny. You have the first turn on the swing."

The tree was high and the rope was long. Penny swung way, way out, before the rope brought her back to the bank.

"It's fun!" She laughed.

Then Pete had his turn.

The tide crept higher and higher until finally there was water, instead of beach, beneath them when they swung far out. The children put on their swimming suits and dragged their feet in the water as they zoomed out. What a big splash. What fun!

"There are lots of ways to have fun," said Penny.

Daddy had been watching her swing. "But there is only one way to get to heaven," he said.

Pete and Penny sat on the bank to rest a minute. "Some people," said Daddy, "think that they can get to heaven by being good."

"But they can't ever be good enough," added Penny.

"Some people," said Daddy, "think that they can get to heaven by joining a church."

"But being a church member won't save them," said Penny.

"Some people," said Daddy, "think that idols can get them to heaven."

"But idols can't see or hear or help. How could they save?" asked Pete.

"Some people," said Daddy, "think that they can get to heaven by giving money to poor people or to the church."

"But you can't buy your way to heaven," said Penny.

"No," said Daddy. Then he read from his little Bible, " 'Jesus saith unto him, I am the way, the

52

truth, and the life: no man cometh unto the Father, but by me' (John 14:6)."

"Jesus is the only way," said Penny. "I am glad Jesus died for me. I am glad I know it, and I am glad I believe it."

Roasted Wieners

WHEN DADDY asked Pete to build a fire, Pete was glad to do it.

Penny helped gather the wood. She carried some in her apron. Then she put a kettle of water on the grate. While the wood burned and the flames died down to coals, Pete and Penny husked corn.

Mother was stirring up biscuit dough in a big bowl. She had no rolling pin at camp, so she divided the dough into little gobs. She rolled one between the palms of her hands and flattened it with her fingers. Then she laid the long strip on a piece of wax paper.

Penny put a lid on the kettle of corn and then helped Mother roll and pat pieces of dough into long, flat strips. She liked the feel of the soft dough between her fingers. Pete helped, too.

After Daddy had been called and they had prayed,

thanking God for the food, each one put a wiener on a stick and roasted it.

"I'm ready for my dough," said Penny.

Mother helped her wind a long strip around the wiener. Then Penny held the wiener in its biscuit dough blanket over the coals and carefully turned it until it was a golden brown.

"It looks and smells good enough to eat," she said as she sat on a log. She had to wait a minute for it to cool. Then she took a big bite.

"Um, it's good." She licked her lips.

Pete and Daddy sat on the same log. When Mother had eaten her wiener, she threw a few pieces of wood on the fire. Soon they burst into flames. The flames licked at the wood, then danced up and down.

"Daddy," asked Pete, "what will happen to people who don't get saved?"

"Say John 3:16 for me, Pete," said Daddy.

So Pete recited the verse:

> For God so loved the world, that he gave his only begotten Son, that whosoever believeth in him should not perish, but have everlasting life (John 3:16).

"The ones who believe won't perish," said Penny. "The ones who don't believe, will perish." Then she puckered up her forehead. "Daddy, what does *perish* mean?"

55

"Perish means to die and go to hell," answered Daddy. "The Bible says, 'the fearful, and unbelieving . . . and all liars shall have their part in the lake which burneth with fire and brimstone: which is the second death' (Revelation 21:8)."

Daddy looked at the flickering flames of the fire. Then he added, "The Bible tells of two men, a beggar and a rich man. The beggar died and went to heaven. 'The rich man also died, and was buried; and in hell he lift up his eyes, being in torments' (Luke 16:22-23)."

"What does *torment* mean?" asked Pete.

"How would it feel to be *in* a flame of fire?" asked Daddy.

Pete looked at the fire but did not answer.

Daddy read more from his Bible:

> He cried and said, Father Abraham, have mercy on me, and send Lazarus, that he may dip the tip of his finger in water, and cool my tongue; for I am tormented in this flame (Luke 16:24).

"I am glad," said Penny, "that God promised that I will not perish if I believe in His Son, the Lord Jesus Christ."

A Little Animal with White Stripes

PETE AND PENNY and Daddy and Mother sat around the fire long after it was dark. After a while, the moon, looking like a big, round, wagon wheel, moved above the tops of the dark fir trees. As it climbed higher in the sky, it made a sparkling path on the water.

They had been singing by the fire. Pete had a mouth organ and could play while the others sang, "What can wash away my sins? Nothing but the blood of Jesus." They sang the song two times.

Then Penny heard a noise. "Listen," she whispered.

The noise came from down on the beach.

Daddy was the first to see the little animal. He pointed.

There, in the light of the moon, was a skunk. It was the same size as their tiger cat, only it had a big, bushy tail. Two white stripes ran down its black back.

"Hold your nose!" cried Pete.

"The skunk won't squirt and smell bad if we don't frighten it," whispered Daddy. "Just sit still and watch."

The skunk sniffed and snuffed around before it

57

scurried past them and disappeared in the shadows of the big trees.

The little family continued to sit on the beach looking at the great star-filled sky above them.

Suddenly Penny wanted to sing "Jesus loves me, this I know, for the Bible tells me so."

When she had finished, Pete asked, "Daddy, if God loves the world, like it says in John 3:16, how come He made hell? Could a God who loves everybody, really send anybody to hell that is full of torments?"

"God is holy; He hates sin," replied Daddy. "He cannot look on sin or be friends with a person who is still in his sins. God made hell for Satan, who tries to destroy men's souls. If any man goes there, it is because he chooses to do so. But God loved people so much that He made it possible for us to get rid of our sin and be friends with Him if we want to. Listen to this verse:

> Herein is love, not that we loved God, but that he loved us, and sent his Son to be the propitiation for our sins (1 John 4:10).

"What is *propitiation?*" asked Pete.

"It means that Jesus did what had to be done so that the holy God and sinful man could be friends again," replied Daddy.

Then Mother spoke. "Each one must choose for himself. When I was nine years old, I became a Christian. My father read this verse to me from the Bible, 'Him that cometh to me I will in no wise cast out' (John 6:37). I came to Jesus in prayer and told Him I was sorry for my sin, and He took me into His family. He promised that if anyone comes to Him, He will not cast him out."

"I came to Him," said Penny. "I have everlasting life. It makes me happy in my heart."

Making Gifts for Their Friends

THE NEXT MORNING Pete and Penny went exploring on the tide flats. Penny wore a pink dress with a full skirt, and Pete wore blue shorts and a blue and white striped shirt. They brought back a bucketful of things they had picked up.

They spread their treasures out on the floor of the tree house and went to work. They had a plan. They would make little presents to give Grandma and Aunt Pat and Janey who lived next door to them in Seattle.

They had a box of crayons and glue and scissors in it.

Penny picked up a sand dollar. It was a flat shell, round and smooth and the size of a big cooky. It had the design of pretty daisy petals on it.

She had seven sand dollars, and on every one was a daisy pattern.

"God must like pretty things to make patterns, even on a shell."

Penny decided to color the flower petals with crayons.

She colored each sand dollar differently, but all were pretty.

Pete did not like to color. He decided to make a long-legged blue heron bird. He found a snail shell for its head, a closed cockleshell for its body, and two halves of mussel shells for its flat feet. In their box of supplies were wires covered with fuzzy thread. These were just what he needed to make the long neck and the two long legs.

Before lunch, Mother and Daddy came to see the pretty presents.

"Grandma will love the sand dollars," said Mother. "She can set them in a row on her fireplace mantel."

"Do you think Aunt Pat will like the blue heron?" asked Pete.

"It looks real enough to gobble a bullhead fish," said Daddy.

61

Then Daddy thought of something. "What if Aunt Pat won't take your gift, Pete? Suppose you put it in a little box and wrap it up and hand it to her; and she says, 'Oh, just put it on the table. I'll look at it later, maybe.' What if she won't even take it from you or say thank you?"

"I'd feel pretty bad," said Pete. "I looked and looked for shells that would be just the right shape to make this blue heron. I spent a lot of time making it. I planned it just for Aunt Pat. I hope she will want it and be pleased."

Daddy had a Bible verse ready to read. " 'For the wages of sin is death, but the gift of God is eternal life through Jesus Christ our Lord' (Romans 6:23)."

Daddy turned back a page in the Bible. "God planned the gift of eternal life," said Daddy. " 'While we were yet sinners, Christ died for us' (Romans 5:8). How do you suppose God feels about people who won't accept the gift He has planned for them?"

"Not very good," answered Pete.

"Tell me," said Daddy, "have you taken God's free gift and said thank you to Him?"

Pete Makes a Dish Garden

PETE WAS THINKING about Daddy's question, but he did not answer right away. Daddy had said, "Tell me, have you taken God's free gift and said thank you to Him?"

Pete could have easily said, "Sure, I have." But Pete was afraid to lie. He wanted to be sure he was telling the truth. He wanted to think about it.

While he was thinking, he was working with his fingers. He picked up a big clamshell. He would make a little dish garden.

"Help me, Daddy," he said. "Come into the woods with me and help me find moss and tiny plants and trees."

So Daddy and Pete left Penny and Mother in the tree house.

Pete found some soft green moss to lay in the big shell. Daddy found a tiny fir tree. A few bell-shaped flowers and a wee huckleberry bush which was only three inches tall was all the shell would hold.

"I'll make a little animal out of shells and let it walk in my woods," said Pete. "The dish garden will be a nice present for Janey who lives next door to us."

Daddy and Pete walked back toward camp.

"Are you ready to answer my question?" asked Daddy.

"I have been going to church all my life," said Pete. "When I was just a tiny baby you took me, and I have gone ever since."

"You know *about* God's gift, Pete, but have you *accepted* it? Have you taken Him as your own Saviour?"

"Aw," said Pete. "We have a Christian family. You are always reading the Bible to us, and we have family devotions every day."

"Having Christian parents doesn't save you, Pete." Daddy opened his Bible and read, " 'Choose life, that . . . thou . . . may live' (Deuteronomy 30:19)."

"God lets each person choose," said Daddy. "Some decide that they don't want to believe in Jesus. Some say that they will wait and do it some other day. Many people put it off too long, and they die without being saved."

Pete looked at his bare feet. "I've never robbed a bank," he said. "I'm not so wicked."

Daddy reminded Pete of the verse he had read before which said that the fearful and unbelieving and all liars would have a second death.

Then Pete remembered the lie he had told long ago to get Penny into trouble. He remembered other lies he had told since then. He knew that being an unbeliever was enough to keep him from having eternal life.

"I will take God's gift of eternal life right now," said Pete. "Ever since I can remember, I have believed in my head that Jesus died for me. Today, this minute, I believe it with all my heart."

There, in the woods, Pete bowed his head. "Dear God," he prayed, "Thank You for sending Jesus to die for *me*."

God Controls the Sea

PETE AND PENNY PENDLETON camped on the beach with their mother and father for two weeks. Each morning when they woke up, the water was way, way out; and there was lots of beach to play on. Each day the ocean rises until its water runs far up on the beach. This is called the tide.

"The tide is out. Let's explore on the beach," Pete suggested.

They splashed in the shallow water and found starfish and dug for clams.

Today Penny wanted to build a castle in the wet

sand. They used shells for a wall and bits of seaweed for a flag. Finally they had a lovely castle.

"The tide," wailed Penny. "The tide is coming in, and it will spoil our castle."

Inch by inch, the water crept up the beach until it touched the castle. Slowly the water swirled around; and as it moved up the beach toward the bank above, the castle was covered bit by bit and finally hidden by the water.

By noon the tide was a few feet from the campfire. But it did not reach the fire. The tide changed, and after a while there was a narrow border of wet stones all around the bay. The border grew from an inch to a foot and wider and wider. The tide was going out again. Most of the afternoon, the water was going out. Then the tide turned. The water came back up the beach slowly, but it came.

Penny had watched the tide go in and out every day. Today, a south wind had sprung up and the waves splashed on the shore.

When it was time to unroll the sleeping bags on the beach, Penny was afraid.

"What if the tide forgets to go out and the water creeps up and up and up onto the beach and covers us all in our sleeping bags while we are asleep, and we are all drowned!"

Daddy felt like laughing, but he didn't. He reached

for his Bible, and Pete and Penny and Mommy listened while he read:

> The LORD . . . placed the sand for the bound of the sea by a perpetual decree, that it cannot pass it: and though the waves thereof toss themselves, yet can they not prevail; though they roar, yet can they not pass over it (Jeremiah 5:22).

Daddy looked at the waves lapping at his feet. "The great Lord God, the Creator of heaven and earth and the sea, He is the One who tells the waves how far they can go and no farther. Listen to this verse." He read from the Bible again.

> The Lord on high is mightier than the noise of many waters, yea, than the mighty waves of the sea (Psalm 93:4).

Then Penny was not afraid to sleep on the beach. But before she slept, she thanked God that He was a mighty God and that He would not let the water go past the place He had planned for it to go.

What the "Fool" Says

IT WAS MORNING. Pete smelled bacon. He jumped out of his sleeping bag. Bacon and eggs and toast, and oranges cut in half! What a good breakfast!

But before they ate, Daddy said, "Pete, will you please thank God for this food?"

Each one bowed his head and shut his eyes.

Then Pete prayed, "Dear God, we thank Thee for this good food. In Jesus' name. Amen."

While Pete was munching bacon, he thought of something.

"When I was over at Bob's house for dinner one day, I waited for someone to pray; but nobody did. I said, 'At our house, we thank God for the food before we eat it.' Do you know what Bob's dad said?"

"What?" asked Penny.

"He said," replied Pete, " 'I earned the money to buy this food. I bought the food. Why should I thank *God* for it?' "

"That man is a fool," said Daddy.

Penny looked shocked. She knew that Daddy and Mommy had told her and Pete that it was not nice to call anybody a fool.

"*I* am not calling him that," said Daddy. "God is."

Daddy pulled his Bible out of his pocket. "Listen to this verse: 'The fool hath said in his heart, there is no God' (Psalm 14:1)."

"The man who thinks *he* earned money and bought food and doesn't need to thank God for it, is saying, 'There is no God. I got this food by working.' God says that man is a fool."

"He forgets," added Mother, "that if God did not send the sunshine and the rain to make plants grow, there would be no carrots or onions or potatoes to buy. If God did not give sunshine and rain, there would be no grass or grain for the cows. Then there would be no meat to eat. There would be no milk to drink."

"Yes," added Pete, "and God gave Bob's dad his health. If he were sick in bed, he couldn't be working to earn money."

"The very air we breathe is a gift from God," said Penny. "We can't live without air."

Daddy had turned to other Bible verses:

> He causeth the grass to grow for the cattle, and herb for the service of man: that he may bring forth food out of the earth . . . and bread which strengtheneth man's heart (Psalm 104:14-15).
>
> O give thanks unto the LORD; for he is good: for his mercy endureth forever . . . who giveth food to all flesh: for his mercy endureth forever (Psalm 136:1, 25).

"Yes," said Pete, "we will thank God for our food, always."

Off on a Hike

WHILE THEY were eating breakfast, Pete had an idea.

"I'll wash the dishes, Mom, while you pack a lunch so we can go on a hike. OK, Mom? Is that OK?"

"Yes, Mother," pleaded Penny. "Let's go on a hike, please. I'll dry the dishes."

Mother smiled. "It is a good idea. Daddy can roll up the sleeping bags, and we'll all be ready to start together."

Pete whistled while he sloshed soapy water on the dishes. Water splashed over the edge of the pan, but it didn't matter. The dishpan was on a big rock on the beach, and the water splashed on the little rocks.

"I must work before I play; that's the way I start my day," sang Penny; and Pete whistled the same tune.

When they were home, Pete and Penny always did a job for Mother before they went out to play. Mother would name the things that had to be done: wash the dishes, sweep the porch, wash fingerprints off the bathroom door, make the beds, and polish the silver. Then she would let them choose the job they wanted to do. Always they sang their little song: "I must work before I play; that's the way I start my day."

Out camping there weren't so many things to do,

but there were dishes to wash. It wouldn't be fair to let mother do all the work on their vacation.

It wasn't long before they were ready to start on the hike. Daddy carried the lunch basket and Pete carried the water jug. They scrambled up the bank and started down a path through the woods.

The sun was shining brightly. It made dancing patterns on the ground as it shone through the fluttering leaves.

The air was fresh and cool. Pete took a deep breath.

"I'm glad I'm alive," he said.

"It is good to be alive," agreed Daddy. "Of all the wonderful things God created, I think that bodies that are alive and can grow are the most wonderful."

Daddy was walking behind Pete, and Penny was walking behind Daddy. Mother came last.

"Did God make me?" asked Penny.

Daddy pulled his Bible from his pocket and found Psalm 100. Pete leaned against a tree and Penny stood staring at Daddy with wide eyes as they listened.

> Know ye that the LORD he is God: it is he that hath made us, and not we ourselves (Psalm 100:3).

"God made the first man out of dirt," explained Daddy. "Listen to these verses."

> So God created man in his own image, in the image of God created he him; male and female created he

73

them (Genesis 1:27). And the LORD God formed man of the dust of the ground, and breathed into his nostrils the breath of life; and man became a living soul (Genesis 2:7).

"It is wonderful," said Mother, "that God breathed into the man He had made out of dust, and that man became a live man who could see and hear and smell and feel. Only God could do that. 'It is He that hath made us, and not we ourselves.' Shall we thank Him, now, that we are alive?"

So they did.

Taste Is from God

"THE HUCKLEBERRIES are all gone," sighed Penny, "and I am hungry." She brushed a brown curl back from her cheek.

"Let's eat lunch," said Daddy.

They sat on a log; and before they ate, they sang,

> Every good gift and ev'ry perfect gift
>   Is from above;
> And cometh down from the Father,
>   From the Father we love.*

Each head was bowed.

Primaries Sing, published by Scripture Press.

"Dear Lord," said Daddy, "we do praise You for this food. Thank You. In Jesus' name. Amen."

Then Mother unpacked the lunch basket. There were tuna fish sandwiches and honey sandwiches and celery sticks and potato chips and big round, rosy, juicy peaches.

Pete took a big bite of a tuna fish sandwich. Soon it was gone. Then he helped himself to a honey sandwich.

"Umm—mm! Tastes good," he said.

"I see you agree with what the Bible says." Daddy laughed.

Pete thought Daddy hadn't understood him. "I wasn't talking about the Bible, Daddy. I only said that this honey tastes good."

"I know," said Daddy. "Let me read you a verse." He slipped his Bible from his pocket.

> My son, eat thou honey, because it is good; and the honeycomb, which is sweet to thy taste (Proverbs 24:13).

Pete smiled. "Well, that's one thing I don't mind doing. It says to eat honey because it is good and it is sweet." He took another honey sandwich when Mother passed it to him, not forgetting to say, thank you.

"Honey is good," said Penny, "but I'm glad every-

75

thing in the wide world doesn't taste like honey." She bit into a peach and tipped her head over so that the juice could drip onto the ground. "This peach is ripe and sweet. It doesn't taste like honey, but it tastes just as good."

"Say, it would be awful if everything tasted the same," agreed Pete. "Let's see how many different tastes we can think of."

"Sour pickles, sweet candy, spicy cookies, salty fish," began Mother.

"I like the taste of roast beef," said Penny, "and watermelon, and corn on the cob, and mush with brown sugar on it, and corn bread with blackberry jam."

"Don't forget how good fried salmon can taste," added Pete, "and cabbage with vinegar on it, and co-conut pudding."

"We can thank God for the gift of taste," said Daddy. Then he read another verse from his little Bible, " 'I will praise thee; for I am fearfully and wonderfully made' (Psalm 139:14)."

Hearing Ears Are Also a Gift

ON A BRANCH overhead sat a tiny brown bird. Pete and Penny and Daddy and Mother were so busy talking that they didn't know it was there.

But when the little bird opened his mouth to let a happy song tumble out, Penny raised her hand and said, "Listen!"

All four listened. There it was again. A whistled tune of bouncing notes that bubbled up, down, then up again.

"I can whistle," said Pete, "but I can't whistle like that."

"What if God had made us without ears to hear?" asked Penny. "It makes me happy to hear that little bird sing."

Daddy knew just where to look for the right Bible verse.

> The hearing ear, and the seeing eye, the LORD hath made even both of them (Proverbs 20:12).

"It is true," said Mother. "We are fearfully and wonderfully made. I am glad that God made the hearing ear."

"That's a funny way to say it. Don't all ears hear?" asked Penny.

"Some people are deaf," replied Mother. "They have ears, but they can't hear."

"Like Grandpa Pendleton?" asked Pete.

"He is partly deaf because he is so old," said Mother. "If you shout, he can hear you. But some people are completely deaf. They can't hear a thing. When people are very sick, sometimes they lose their hearing."

"I'm glad I have hearing ears," said Penny. "I'm glad I can hear you talk to me, and I like to hear the wind sighing in the treetops. At night I like to hear the water lapping on the rocks."

"I like to hear accordion music," said Pete, "and the hum my top makes; and I like to hear our tiger cat purr. I'm glad I have hearing ears."

"I'm glad," said Daddy, "that I have ears to hear about God. In the Bible it says that some people turn away their ears from the truth. They won't go to church where they can hear that Jesus is the only way to heaven. They want to hear lies and believe them. I'm glad I have hearing ears, and I want to use my ears to listen to things that will make me love God more."

"Jesus is in heaven now," said Mother, "but He has promised to come back again. 'Then . . . the ears of the deaf shall be unstopped' (Isaiah 35:5)."

"That's good," said Penny. "Hearing ears are a wonderful gift from God."

Then she looked up and listened to the little brown bird sing his happy song once more before he flew away.

A Nose to Smell Flowers

AFTER LUNCH, Pete and Penny and Daddy and Mother walked on down the path. It led them in a loop, and after awhile they were back on the bank above the beach not far from their camp.

Penny clutched a fistful of flowers. In the deep woods she had found tiny, pink, bell-shaped flowers that pushed themselves up from a mossy bed. In the open sunny stretches were patches of wild sweet peas —some a pinky purple, some white. In the dry rocky places above the beach were white daisies with yellow centers.

Back at camp, Penny filled a tin can with water and put the flowers in it.

She had been sniffing at them all the way back. Now she poked her nose into them one more time, before putting them on the picnic table.

"They smell so sweet," she said with a big sigh.

"I love to look at flowers, but I love to smell them even more."

Mother liked the verse that Daddy had read from his little Bible in the woods, so she said it again: " 'I will praise thee; for I am fearfully and wonderfully made' (Psalm 139:14)." Then she added, "Smell is a gift from God. We should thank Him for it."

"Yes, there are lots of nice smells," agreed Penny. "I like the smell of an orange and the smell of the salt air here by the beach and—"

While Penny tried to think of some more smells that she liked, Daddy spoke up. "I like to open the kitchen door and smell cookies baking, and I like the smell of hay in a barn, and I like the smell of cedar wood when I saw boards."

Pete sat on the log beside Daddy and tossed a stone into the water. "Some smells aren't so nice, though. The smell of smoke chokes me and makes me cough."

"The smell of smoke has saved many lives," Daddy reminded. "What if fire would burn, but the smoke from it had no smell at all? The smell of smoke is a warning that fire is near, and it warns you to run— unless of course the fire is in a fireplace where it belongs."

"When I have a cold," said Penny, "I can't smell anything and I can't taste anything either. It always makes me sad to sit down with a good dinner in front of me if I can't smell how good it is and if everything tastes the same."

"Our senses of smelling and tasting are closely connected," agreed Mother.

Penny sniffed at her bouquet once more.

"I'm glad I have a 'smelling nose,' " she said. "The Bible says God made the hearing ear and the seeing eye. I'm glad for both of them and also for a nose to smell sweet smells."

God Gave Us Feeling

PETE WENT into the tent and came back wearing his swimming trunks. He sprawled on a warm sandy spot where there were no rocks, and closed his eyes.

He could hear a kingfisher bird screech as it swooped down and dived into the water after a fish. He could smell salty seaweed that the last tide had strewn in a rim on the beach. He could feel the warm sun on his back.

"The sun feels good," he murmured. "It makes me feel lazy and sleepy."

Penny, in her bathing suit, was wading at the

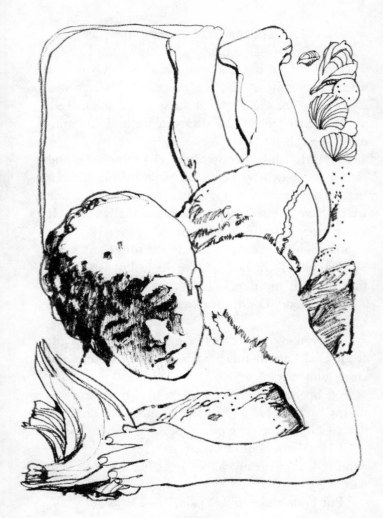

water's edge. "The sun feels warm on my back," she said, "but the water is cold."

Penny waded out until the water was up to her waist. Suddenly she ducked under. The water was so cold that she squealed, but she splashed and kicked.

"It doesn't feel so bad after you are in a few minutes," she called.

In a little while, Penny came out of the water and sat on the beach by Pete. Salt water dripped from her brown hair and down her back, and no one would have guessed that her hair was really curly. It was plastered flat against her head.

She wiggled her toes and dug them into the sand. "It feels good," she said. "I like the feel of sand trickling through my toes."

Mother and Daddy were still sitting on the log nearby.

"Did you ever think that being able to *feel* is a gift from God, just as much as being able to hear and smell and taste?" asked Mother.

Pete opened his eyes. "I like to feel the warm sun on my back, and at night I like to sit by our campfire and feel its warm glow on my face."

"I like the feel of our tiger cat's fur," said Penny, "and I like to wear my velvet dress, because it feels so soft."

"But I don't like to feel pain," said Pete.

Daddy spoke up. "Pain is a blessing, Pete. If you have a pain in your stomach, it is a warning that something is wrong and that maybe you ought to go to the doctor."

"Or," said Mother, laughing, "maybe you shouldn't eat any more green apples."

"That is a warning, too," Daddy agreed.

Mother slipped her hand into Daddy's pocket and took out his Bible and read, " 'O give thanks unto the Lord; for he is good' (Psalm 136:1)."

"I'm glad," said Penny, "that God made me so I can hear and smell and taste—and I'm glad I can *feel*, too. I will give thanks to the Lord for everything He has given me to enjoy."

He Gives the Seeing Eye

DADDY ASKED Pete to build a fire.

Pete knew how to crumple up the paper first and then lay little sticks on the paper, and last of all put big sticks on top. There was plenty of driftwood along the beach. So Pete gathered wood, and he even had enough for a pile to burn later.

When this was done, Daddy came over and watched while Pete struck a match on a stone and held it to the paper. The paper caught on fire. The flames licked at the wood. Soon the little pieces were burning and these started the big pieces. Pete stood and watched. He loved to build a fire. That was why Daddy always called him when there was a fire to build.

Pete knew that he was never, never to build a fire unless Daddy asked him to. He was never, never to strike a match unless Daddy or Mother was there to watch him.

Fire is something which God gave man so that he can cook food and get warm when he is cold. But fire can get out of control and burn buildings and children and make lots of people sad. That is why Pete obeyed Daddy and built fires only when he was asked to do so.

The children roasted wieners in the fire, and Penny sat on the log to eat hers. She looked toward the west. Huge snowcapped mountains, dark blue against the pale blue sky, loomed beyond the bay.

As she watched, the sky changed. The sun was slowly slipping down behind the mountains. At first, the pale blue of the sky changed to a rosy pink, and then gradually the pink grew deeper until the sky was red and the few clouds that floated there were a brilliant, bright orange.

"Look," breathed Penny. "God is painting a sunset for us. I'm glad I can see. Read the verse, Daddy, about the seeing eye."

So Daddy read, " 'The hearing ear, and the seeing eye, the LORD hath made even both of them' (Proverbs 20:12)."

"What if I couldn't see you face, Mother, or bright flowers or swaying green trees or dancing waves," said Penny. "What if the whole world were black both day and night. What if I could hear and taste and smell and feel, but couldn't see? I'm glad I have seeing eyes."

Mother said softly, " 'O give thanks unto the LORD; for he is good' (Psalm 136:1)."

Pete and Penny Dig Clams

THE NEXT MORNING, Pete was the first to wake up. He propped himself on one elbow and looked down the beach. The tide was out. That gave Pete an idea.

"Penny, wake up. Daddy, wake up. Let's dig clams before breakfast."

"It's too early. Let me alone," groaned Penny; and she turned over.

"We have to dig clams while the tide is out.

Come on." Pete poked at Penny and bothered Daddy until they were up.

Down the beach they went, carrying buckets and shovels.

Pete looked for little holes in the sand, holes made by clams squirting water. When he found five together, he started to dig. He didn't have to dig very deep. About six inches down, he found a clam.

Penny picked up the clam, and it made a clicking noise when she dropped it into the pail.

Pete dug, and Penny picked up the clams.

Daddy dug nearby, too.

"Dig lots," said Penny. "I can eat twenty at one meal."

"Not twenty clams!"

"Well, almost twenty."

So Pete and Daddy dug and dug.

"Daddy," said Penny, "if God can see us day or night, no matter where we are, can He hear us anytime, too?"

Daddy stood up and leaned on the shovel handle. "I will answer you with a Bible verse," he said:

> For there is not a word in my tongue, but, lo, O LORD, thou knowest it altogether (Psalm 139:4).

Daddy turned over another shovelful of sand. Then he went on. "God knows every word you say.

He even knows everything you think. You say lots of things I don't hear. I don't know anything you think unless you tell me. But here is a verse to remember."

> The LORD knoweth the thoughts of man, that they are vanity (Psalm 94:11).

"What does *vanity* mean, Daddy?" Penny asked. "God knows our thoughts, and He knows that many of them are vain thoughts. We are proud and selfish and hateful. We don't want other people to know what we are like inside. So many times we pretend to be nice, but our thoughts are really bad. We should ask God to help us think right things, as King David did."

> Search me, O God, and know my heart: try me, and know my thoughts: And see if there be any wicked way in me, and lead me in the way everlasting (Psalm 139:23-24).

"I want to ask God," declared Penny, "to help me think right thoughts."

Penny Makes Sizzling Pancakes

PETE AND PENNY and Daddy carried the clams they had dug back to the camp. Mother was beating pancake batter.

"Let me fry the pancakes, please, Mother. May I?" teased Penny.

"Do you think you can, without burning them?" asked Mother, handing her the pancake turner.

"I've watched you lots of times," said Penny. She tied a blue apron over her blue-checked dress.

"Watching and doing are two different things, but I'll help you," said Mother.

Penny dabbed a little bacon grease into the frying pan. The she put two spoonfuls of batter in the center of the pan and waited.

"When the pancake looks all bubbly, it's time to turn it, isn't it?"

Mother was poking at the campfire under the grate.

"That's right."

The bubbles began to pop. When there were bubbles all over, Penny slipped the pancake turner under and turned one pancake. On the other side, it was a golden brown.

"This is fun," said Penny. "I'll fry all the pancakes for breakfast. Pete," she called. "Oh, Pete."

Pete was pouring oatmeal into the bucket of clams, which was already filled with salt water. That was so the clams would spit out their sand to eat the oatmeal. Then when the family ate clams for supper, they wouldn't feel sand grating between their teeth.

"Pete, I'm frying pancakes. You and Daddy can come."

While they were eating, Pete said, "If we can't hide from God because He sees everything, and if He hears every word we say and even knows what we are thinking, I guess there isn't a thing in the world He doesn't know."

"You guessed right," said Daddy. He wiped his fingers on his napkin and took his Bible from his pocket. He read, " 'God . . . knoweth all things' (1 John 3:20)."

Then he turned to another scripture verse and put the Bible in front of Pete. Pete read where Daddy pointed:

> Are not two sparrows sold for a farthing? and one of them shall not fall on the ground without your Father. But the very hairs of your head are all numbered (Matthew 10:29-30).

"There are lots of sparrows in the world, and they aren't worth much; but God even knows when one of them dies," explained Daddy.

"And to think that God knows how many hairs there are on my head!" exclaimed Penny. "A few came out when I combed my hair, but still God knows how many are left. That's something I could never do. I could never count the hairs on my head."

Daddy had found a verse for Penny to read. He pointed while she read:

> He telleth the number of the stars; he calleth them all by their names. Great is our LORD, and of great power: his understanding is infinite (Psalm 147:4-5).

"God made the stars and He even knows their names," said Daddy.

"What does *infinite* mean?" asked Penny.

"It means no limit. God understands everything. There is not one thing in this world that God doesn't know about or understand. We have a great God."

"He knows everything," said Pete.

How Sea Gulls Open Clams

THE NEXT MORNING, Pete and Penny were sitting on the beach. Penny was pretty in her green dress, the color of madroña leaves. It made her brown eyes look browner.

93

"Look at that sea gull," Pete shouted. "Watch it."

The big bird had picked up a clam from the beach with his beak. Up, up flew the sea gull. Then he dropped the clam on the rocky part of the beach, and it broke open. Down he swooped and began to feast on the clam.

"What a smart bird!" said Penny. "How does he know enough to open a clam that way?"

"I guess God, who made sea gulls, made them know how to get food," said Pete.

The children watched other sea gulls feast on clams the same way.

Daddy came back from a trip to the store. He was told about the sea gulls, and he saw two of them break the clamshells.

"Jesus spent many hours near the shore of the Sea of Galilee," said Daddy. "It was there that He fed five thousand men, besides women and children, with only five buns and two small fishes."

"I know that story," said Pete. "A boy about my size took a lunch along and went to hear Jesus talk to the people. It got late and everyone was hungry, but there wasn't food for that crowd."

"The little boy," interrupted Penny, "gave his lunch to Jesus."

"Jesus prayed," continued Pete. "Then He broke

95

the five loaves and two fishes into pieces, and there was enough food so everyone was filled."

"There were even twelve full baskets left over," added Penny. "But tell me, Daddy, how could Jesus feed so many people with one little boy's lunch?"

"Jesus is the Son of God," answered Daddy. "He can do anything. Feeding all those people was a miracle. A miracle is something that only God can do. Jesus is God's Son. He did many miracles while He was on this earth, to prove to people that He was God's Son."

"I know another miracle Jesus did," said Penny. "A man named Jairus had a little girl who was twelve years old, and she died. Her daddy ran and got Jesus, and He took her by the hand and made her alive again."

"That was a miracle, all right!" said Daddy. "Only God's Son could make a dead girl alive again. Peter, who was one of Jesus' friends, saw Him perform many miracles. For many weeks Peter watched Him and listened to Him talk. One day he said to Jesus, 'We believe and are sure that thou art that Christ, the Son of the living God' (John 6:69)."

"I believe it, too," said Penny. "I believe that Jesus is the Son of God."

They Sent the Gospel in Bottles

PETE AND PENNY walked along the beach where the tide had left a line of bark and other things. Usually there were treasures tucked in the seaweed. Pete poked some seaweed with a stick.

"Boy, just what I need," said Pete, as he picked up something.

"What's so wonderful about an old shingle?" asked Penny.

"Wait. You'll see."

"Here's a bottle with a cork in it." Penny kicked the bottle with her foot.

"Let's keep the bottle. Let's find some more bottles," said Pete.

"We can put story tracts in them, that tell people how to be saved and have everlasting life. If we throw the bottles into the water, they might drift to where someone will find them."

So Pete and Penny looked for bottles with corks or lids. They found three.

Back at camp, Daddy and Mother helped the children to roll up story tracts tightly so they could poke them inside the bottle necks. They put four tracts into each bottle. They also put a little note with the tracts. Each note said, "If you find this please write to Pete and Penny Pendleton at 105 West 200th Street, Seattle, Washington. We threw this bottle into Liberty Bay August 21. We hope you like the stories and do what they say."

Daddy and Pete pushed the boat into the water and all three climbed in. Daddy said Penny could row. Out toward the deep channel she rowed. There the tide swirled more swiftly around the point as the water moved past an island and on toward the Sound, on its way to the big Pacific Ocean.

Pete and Penny each threw a bottle into the water.

"You may have a turn," said Penny. "Here, Daddy, you throw in the last bottle."

So Daddy did.

"Maybe someone will be saved and have everlasting life, because we did this today," said Pete.

Daddy looked at Penny. "Where are you going after you die, Penny?"

"To heaven, I hope."

"I don't *hope* I am going to heaven," said Daddy.

Penny looked surprised.

"Do you have everlasting life?" asked Daddy.

"I hope so," said Penny.

"Listen while I say John 3:16. Tell me where I say it wrong: 'For God so loved the world that He gave His only begotten Son that whosoever believeth in Him should not perish, but hopes he has ever-lasting life.' "

Penny's brown eyes sparkled. "Not *hopes*, Daddy. It says '*have* everlasting life.' "

Daddy popped a piece of candy into Penny's mouth.

"Do you hope you have candy in your mouth?"

"I *have* candy in my mouth," mumbled Penny. "And I *have* everlasting life because I believe that Jesus died for me."

Pete said softly a verse that Daddy had taught him, " 'Verily, verily, I say unto you, He that believeth on me hath everlasting life' (John 6:47)."

Pete and Penny Explore the Woods

PETE AND PENNY explored along the bank above the beach. They decided to collect as many different kinds of leaves and berries as they could. Penny tied the four ends of her scarf together to make a bag to carry their collection.

After they had explored along the bank and into

the edge of the woods, they went back to the beach and spread all their collection on the picnic table.

Daddy was sitting there reading a magazine. "How many kinds can you name?" he asked.

"This is a fir, the kind we get for Christmas trees," said Pete. "And this flat twig is hemlock. The one with long needles is pine."

"The shiny green leaves and bright red berries are from a madrona," Penny added. "And here's a thistle. Even if it is a weed, I like its soft purple flower that looks like a brush."

"I know one thing," said Daddy. "This bunch of blue grapes didn't come off the thorn or thistle."

"Are those grapes?" asked Penny.

"They are wild grapes, Penny," Daddy told her. "They're called Oregon grapes. Being tart, they make good jelly." Then Daddy opened his Bible. "Let me read you what the Bible says about thistles and grapes."

> Do men gather grapes of thorns, or figs of thistles? Even so every good tree bringeth forth good fruit; but a corrupt tree bringeth forth evil fruit. A good tree cannot bring forth evil fruit, neither can a corrupt tree bring forth good fruit . . . Wherefore by their fruits ye shall know them (Matthew 7:16-20).

Then Daddy explained, "You don't gather grapes

101

off thorns. Thorns have no fruit on them, only prickles. A good peach tree will have good peaches on it. A good apple tree will have good apples on it."

"But some trees have nothing but little red berries that aren't good for people to eat," said Pete.

"That is the way with our lives," continued Daddy. "You can tell what people are like by the things they do. If you see a boy sharing his sailboat with his friend, you know he is kind and unselfish."

"If you see a girl scratch and bite another girl," said Penny, "you know she is mean and hateful."

"By their fruits," Daddy went on, "you can tell if a tree is good or not. By the things we do, people can tell if we love God and belong to Him."

"I want to live and act and speak," said Pete, "so that everybody will know I am a Christian boy."

"Sometimes I forget and feel like acting mean," admitted Penny, "but I'll ask the Lord to help me be like a good tree with good fruit. I'll ask Him to help me think and say and do the right things."

A Bunch of Green Grapes

PETE AND PENNY were hungry.

"What may we nibble on, Mother?" asked Penny.

"Green grapes," said Mother. "Here is a bunch of green grapes. They are sweet and juicy. You'll like them."

"Thank you," said Penny. "I do like fruit. I like apples and oranges and peaches and pears, and I like grapes." She popped one into her mouth.

"God made fruit for you to enjoy," Mother said. "And He, too, wants to enjoy fruit—a different kind, though. He is looking at your life, to see if He finds good fruit there."

Penny laughed. "I'm not a peach tree!"

Mother knew where to turn in the Bible and find the right verse:

> But the fruit of the Spirit is love, joy, peace, longsuffering, gentleness, goodness, faith, meekness, temperance (Galatians 5:22, 23).

"God," she said, "is looking for the fruit of the Spirit in your life. We have one God, Penny, but our wonderful God is three Persons. God the Father planned how we could be saved. God the Son died in our place so that we could be saved. God the Holy Spirit helps you to know that you need to be saved, and He helps you to understand the Bible and to live so that your life will bear the right kind of fruit."

Mother picked up a bunch of grapes. "Shall we let each grape stand for a fruit of the Spirit that God is looking for in our lives? One will be love, another will be joy, and others will be peace, longsuffering, gentleness, goodness, faith, meekness, and temperance, or self-control."

"Some of those words I can't understand," said Penny.

"Sometime I'll explain each one to you," replied Mother. "Right now I want to read what Jesus said about the greatest commandment of all. A long, long time ago, God gave His people ten commandments. They were rules to help them to live good lives. When Jesus came to earth, He put them together into two commandments."

> Thou shalt love the Lord thy God with all thy heart, and with all thy soul, and with all thy mind. This is the first and great commandment. And the second is like unto it, Thou shalt love thy neighbor as thyself (Matthew 22:37-39).

"If you love God with all your heart," Daddy explained, "and if you love your neighbor as much as you love yourself, then all the fruit of joy and peace and goodness will show forth from your life."

"It's hard to love somebody else, like your neighbor, or even your sister," said Pete, "as much as you love yourself. It's just natural to want the biggest piece of cake and the best bunch of grapes for yourself."

"No matter how much we try, we can never make the fruit of the Spirit grow in our lives," said Daddy. "But if we often ask the Lord to do it for us, and believe that He will, He will help us. God the Holy Spirit is waiting and wanting to help us as soon as we ask Him."

"I will ask Him," said Pete. "I'll ask God to help me love other people as much as I love myself."

Off for Home

PETE AND PENNY helped Daddy to pull up the tent stakes. Their vacation was over, and it was time to go home. Mother packed the dishes and the food. Daddy folded the tent while Pete and Penny let the air out of their air mattresses. There were lots of things to pack and get ready to go. They all had fun together. Now they were working together.

Penny stacked her seashell dishes and looked around at the tree house for the last time.

"I hate to leave." She sighed. "I have been so happy here." She brushed a brown curl back from her face.

Daddy was tying the canvas case around the folded tent. "What is happiness?" he asked.

Pete was kneeling on his sleeping bag. He was trying to roll it tightly. "Why, when you are happy," he said, "you have everything you want. You can't think of another thing you need to make you feel better. That's what happiness is."

Daddy put the tent pole into the car trunk. Then he asked, "What do most people think they need to make them really happy?"

"Money," said Penny. "Lots of money. Mr. Barber, who lives next door at home, has lots of money."

"Is he happy?" asked Daddy.

"No," said Pete. "Mr. Barber has a big green house and a big red car and a big white sailboat and lots of clothes and rings and everything money can buy, but he isn't happy."

"How do you know he isn't happy?" Daddy wanted to know.

"Well," said Pete, "he never seems satisfied. He's always looking for something new to buy or some new place to go."

"He goes lots of places, but he never goes to church," said Penny. "He doesn't read his Bible or love God. He even hates God. He told me so."

"Do you think," asked Daddy, "that a person can be poor and still be happy?"

Before anyone could answer, Daddy opened his little Bible.

107

But godliness with contentment is great gain. For we brought nothing into this world, and it is certain we can carry nothing out. And having food and raiment let us be therewith content. But they that will be rich fall into temptation and a snare, . . . For the love of money is the root of all evil: . . . But thou, O man of God, flee these things; and follow after righteousness, godliness, faith, love, patience, meekness (1 Timothy 6:6-11).

"Why," said Penny, "those are the fruits of the Spirit."

"Yes," said Daddy. "The only way to be happy is to be a friend of God by taking the Lord Jesus Christ as your very own Saviour and then trusting Him every day to help you live for Him."

"As God says," Mother smiled, "none of us brought anything into this world. When we die, we cannot take a single thing from this earth with us."

Pete had been thinking. "But we *need* money," he said. "We can't buy food or clothes or anything without money."

"We do need money," agreed Daddy. "But when a person loves money *more* than anything else, he gets into trouble. 'Godliness with contentment is great gain.' That means if we love God and are content with what He gives us or doesn't give us, then we have happiness which money can't buy."

"I have been happy here," said Penny. "I hate to leave our camp, but I'll be happy anywhere now because I love Jesus."

A Ride on the Ferryboat

PETE AND PENNY stood on the top deck of the ferry and watched the cars drive up the plank. When the last car was on the ferry, a man closed the gate at the end of the dock. The captain pulled a rope that jingled a bell in the engine room. The big engines began to chug. The ferry whistle shrieked. Sea gulls screeched. The water churned and foamed, and they were off!

"A ferry ride is fun," said Pete.

The ferry turned out of the tiny harbor where the dock was located and chugged into the big bay. Pete and Penny walked with Daddy and Mother up to the bow.

"It's a good thing," said Penny, "that our vacation is ending. We had good weather most of the time. But look at those clouds, Pete! They're black."

"The wind here in the bay is pretty strong," said Pete. "It pushes me so I have to lean against it to keep from being blown down."

"I like ferryboat rides in nice weather," said Penny. "But I don't like storms. Daddy, this ferry is beginning to bounce."

"As soon as the captain heads the ferry toward our dock, we won't bounce; we'll roll."

"I'm afraid," said Penny. "Hold my hand, Daddy. I can't stand up straight. I take a step, and the ferry leans over, and I walk like a drunken man."

"Let's pray," said Pete. "Let's ask the Lord to help the ferry get to the other dock safely."

So they all sat on a bench; and Daddy prayed, "Dear God, You know how hard the wind is blowing. All four of us belong to You because each of us has taken Jesus as his Saviour. So we know You'll hear us when we pray to You. Please help the ferry to dock safely. In Jesus' name. Amen."

Penny looked up. "The wind is still blowing. The ferry's still rolling."

"Faith is an important fruit of the Spirit," Daddy reminded her. "We asked God to take care of us. We must believe that He will, even if the wind seems as strong as before we prayed."

Then Daddy turned to a place in his Bible:

> They that go down to the sea in ships, that do business in great waters; these see the works of the Lord, and his wonders in the deep. For he commandeth, and raiseth the stormy wind, which lifteth up the waves

thereof. They mount up to the heaven, they go down again to the depths: their soul is melted because of trouble. They reel to and fro, and stagger like a drunken man, and are at their wit's end. Then they cry unto the Lord in their trouble, and he bringeth them out of their distresses. He maketh the storm a calm, so that the waves thereof are still. Then are they glad because they be quiet; so he bringeth them unto their desired haven. Oh that men would praise the Lord for his goodness, and for his wonderful works to the children of men! (Psalm 107:23-31).

Pete looked up. "The boat isn't rolling so much. The wind doesn't seem so strong."

"We are nearly at the dock," said Daddy.

"God heard our prayer and took care of us," said Penny, gratefully.

A Surprise from Bob and Janey

PETE AND PENNY were glad to get back home. It was fun to go away, and it was fun to be back.

Tiger cat was happy to see them. He arched his back and rubbed against their legs and purred.

"Did Bob Barber feed you every day?" asked Pete. "You look fat and happy."

Then Pete and Penny went next door to find Janey

111

and Bob. They wanted to thank them for feeding tiger cat, and they wanted to talk to them. They always liked to play with Janey and Bob.

Janey saw them coming.

"Bob!" Janey shrieked. "Here come those horrid twins!"

Pete and Penny thought she was teasing.

But Bob bounced out of the door and stared with a scowl on his face.

"Thanks for taking care of tiger cat," said Pete.

Bob dug the toe of his shoe into the dirt. "Well, I had to, didn't I? I promised. Couldn't let the critter starve."

"Next time you can get somebody else to feed your crazy old cat," Janey yelled. Then she stuck out her tongue at Pete and Penny.

The twins could hardly believe their ears and eyes. "What's the matter?" Pete asked. "I thought we were friends."

"We were, but we aren't anymore," sneered Janey. "Dad doesn't want us to be friends with kids that are dumb enough to believe the Bible."

"There's the fence," Bob said. "You stay on your side and we'll stay on ours." He shook his fist at them. "Go on! I mean it!"

Something hurt inside of Pete, and Penny almost

cried. How could it be? The friends they used to play with, hated them just because they loved God.

As they went in their door, they heard Janey call, "Pete and Penny think they're smart. They go to church and we don't need to. Our daddy says so! Ha, ha, ha!"

"Daddy," wailed Pete. "They hate us because we love God."

"Now you can just give your dish garden made in a shell to someone else," cried Penny. Her brown eyes flashed. "If Janey is so hateful, don't give it to her."

Daddy took his big Bible from the table.

> Love your enemies, bless them that curse you, do good to them that hate you, and pray for them which despitefully use you, and persecute you; that ye may be the children of your Father which is in heaven (Matthew 5:44-45).

Then he explained, "The next verse tells us that if we love only the people who love us, we aren't especially pleasing the Lord. The hard thing for us is to love our enemies and to do something good for those who hate us."

"How can anybody love a nasty red-headed girl who says mean things and tells you to go back on your own side of the fence?" demanded Penny.

"*You* can't," said Daddy, "if you try to by yourself. Love, real love that includes an enemy like Janey, is a fruit of the Spirit. God will give you love for her if you really want Him to and ask Him to."

So Penny prayed, "Dear God, Janey used to be our friend and now she is mean and nasty. Help me to love her anyway. In Jesus' name. Amen." Then she felt better.

Then Pete prayed, too. He asked God to help him love both Bob and Janey. Then he felt better.

A Dish Garden for Janey

THE PRETTY DISH GARDEN in a shell, which Pete had made for Janey, was on the tiny table in the front room. Pete stared at it. Should he take it over to Janey, even if she hated him? She was swinging in her yard. Through the window he could see her red curls fly back from her face.

"Are you really going to give it to her?" asked Penny.

"I suppose I should, but I don't feel much like it," admitted Pete.

Daddy opened his big Bible and read," 'My little

children, let us not love in word, neither in tongue; but in deed and in truth' (1 John 3:18)."

"I guess you'll have to." Penny sighed. "We can't just pray and then *say* we love her and not *do* something to prove it."

"But she'll probably stop swinging and scream at us if she sees us open the gate," said Pete.

Pete wasn't in any hurry to take the dish garden with its soft green moss and little fir tree and tiny huckleberry bush over to Janey. He was glad when he saw Daddy find another place in his big Bible. He listened as Daddy read.

> Beloved, let us love one another: for love is of God; and every one that loveth is born of God, and knoweth God . . . In this was manifested the love of God toward us, because that God sent his only begotten Son into the world, that we might live through him. Herein is love, not that we loved God, but that he loved us, and sent his Son to be the propitiation for our sins. Beloved, if God so loved us, we ought also to love one another (1 John 4:7, 9-11).

"Jesus died for Janey the same as He did for me," Pete said softly, "only she doesn't believe it. If I am nice to her, even when she acts mean, maybe she'll want to be saved."

Pete picked up the dish garden. "That settles it," he said. "Come on, Penny. That Bible verse doesn't

116

mean just our brother. We have to love the kids next door, too."

Janey watched Pete and Penny walk toward her gate.

"Pete and Penny Pendleton!" she screeched. "Get out! This is private property."

But Pete and Penny kept right on. Pete unfastened the gate and they went through. As Pete turned to walk toward Janey, a stone struck his hand. He almost dropped the dish garden.

It is hard, he thought, *to love a girl like that.* Then he sent up a quick prayer. "Help me, dear God," he whispered.

Janey was looking for another stone to throw.

"Janey," called Pete, "I brought you a present. Here. It is a dish garden in a shell."

"He made it just for you," said Penny.

Janey stared. She could hardly believe the twins. But she dropped her stone and took the dish garden which Pete held out to her.

"Thanks," she mumbled. Then her face became red and she ran into her house.

"We did our best to be friends," said Penny. "We'll have to pray hard that Janey will know that we love her and that God loves her, too."

The Twins Write an Invisible Message

"PETE," SAID PENNY, "I know a good way to write a message. It is mysterious."

"Mysterious? What do you mean?"

"We will write a note to Bob and Janey; and when they get it, it will look like a plain piece of paper with nothing written on it. Then if they do what we tell them, they can read a message on that same paper."

"Do you know what you are talking about?" asked Pete.

"Sure, follow me."

Penny asked Mother for a lemon. Then she squeezed the juice and poured it into an empty pill bottle.

"Get a toothpick and some paper," she told Pete. Then she sat at the desk. "What message shall we send?"

"Tell them to meet us at the cave right after lunch to play "Pirates" like we used to there," replied Pete.

Penny dipped the toothpick into the lemon juice and wrote what Pete had said.

"They can't read that," Pete protested. "I can't, and neither can you."

"That is the mystery. The message is hidden; but

if they will hold the letter near a warm place or run a hot iron over it, they can read it."

On the envelope she wrote, "Hold this paper in a warm place or iron it. Read, and do what it says."

Pete slipped it under the Barbers' door, rang the doorbell, and ran.

After school, Pete and Penny hurried to the cave. "Bob and Janey must have made the mysterious letter talk," said Pete. "Here they come."

"That letter was fun," Janey said. "Tomorrow we will write one to you if you tell us how." She opened a bag and took out apples and cookies. "Bob and I are glad you still want to be friends."

That evening Pete and Penny told Daddy and Mother all about it.

"I will tell you about another mystery," began Daddy. "Paul wrote about it in the Bible, in a letter to the Christians at Corinth."

> Behold, I show you a mystery; We shall not all sleep, but we shall all be changed, in a moment, in the twinkling of an eye, at the last trump: for the trumpet shall sound, and the dead shall be raised incorruptible, and we shall be changed (1 Corinthians 15:51-52).

"When it says," explained Daddy, "that we shall not all sleep, it means we won't all die. Jesus is coming back someday to get those who believe He is the Son of God who died and rose again for them. The trumpet will sound, and the dead people who were saved by believing in Jesus before they died will come alive."

"What does *incorruptible* mean?" asked Penny.

"It means that the Lord Jesus Christ will give us new bodies that won't ever be sick or die," replied Daddy. "We will all be changed."

"I hope I am alive when Jesus comes back," Pete said, "so I won't have to die."

"The main thing is to be ready," said Daddy. "If you believe that the Lord Jesus Christ died for your sins and you are saved, you are ready to die or to go with Jesus if He comes first."

"I am ready," said Pete. "Since last summer I've believed that Jesus died for my sins."

"I am ready, too," Penny said. "I'm glad I am ready."

News About Grandpa Pendleton

PETE AND PENNY heard the telephone ring very early the next morning. Daddy answered it.

"He did?" Daddy's voice sounded sad. "Last night around eleven? . . . I'll come as soon as I can."

After Daddy hung up the receiver, he turned to Pete and Penny. "Grandpa Pendleton died last night."

"Grandpa dead?" asked Penny. "Next time we drive to Oregon, won't grandpa be there?"

Daddy did not answer for a few minutes. He was thinking about the sad news. "No," he said, "Grandpa isn't alive anymore. His body is still there, but the real person who lived inside that body is gone."

"Where is grandpa, really?" asked Pete.

"With God," answered Daddy. "The Bible tells us that when saved people die, they are absent from the body but present with the Lord."

"Grandpa Pendleton was a Christian," Penny said. "He always prayed for us."

"The funeral will be on Wednesday," Daddy told them. "They will put grandpa's body in a casket, a big box covered with soft cloth. The preacher will read from the Bible so all the friends and relatives will not be so sad. Then they will put the big box in a hole in the ground and cover it with dirt."

"Grandpa Pendleton is dead!" Penny sighed. "Daddy, he was your daddy. You aren't crying."

"I feel sad," said Daddy. "I will miss my father, but he is happy in heaven with God and His Son, the Lord Jesus Christ." Then Daddy opened his Bible and read several verses:

But I would not have you to be ignorant, brethren, concerning them which are asleep, that ye sorrow not, even as others which have no hope. For if we believe that Jesus died and rose again, even so them also which sleep in Jesus will God bring with him. For this we say unto you by the word of the Lord, that we which are alive and remain unto the coming of the Lord shall not prevent them which are asleep. For the Lord himself shall descend from heaven with a shout, with the voice of the archangel, and with the trump of God: and the dead in Christ shall rise first: Then we which are alive and remain shall be caught up together with them in the clouds, to meet the Lord in the air: and so shall we ever be with the Lord. Wherefore comfort one another with these words (1 Thessalonians 4:13-18).

Pete and Penny sat on a stool and listened.

"When the trumpet of God blares out," Daddy went on, "all the dead people who believed in Jesus and were saved from their sins will rise from the dead. God will change those worn-out corruptible bodies into new bodies, and the spirit that has been with God will go into that new body. Then you and I, if we are still alive, will be caught up in the clouds; and we will meet the Lord Jesus Christ in the air. It is the day we all are waiting for."

Mother started to pack Daddy's suitcase so he could go to Oregon to the funeral.

"If grandpa had not been a Christian, it would be very sad, wouldn't it?" asked Pete.

"Very sad," said Daddy. "A person must be saved before he dies. After that, it is too late."

"I am glad I am saved," said Penny. "I am glad I will see Jesus someday."

Daddy Returns at Last

PETE AND PENNY looked out of the window once more.

"When do you suppose he will come?" asked Penny. "We thought Daddy would come back from Oregon yesterday, and he didn't. All day today we have watched and waited. We set his plate at the table at noon in case he came. Mother made some pudding with fruit in it for dessert tonight, because he likes it. Do you think he will come by suppertime?"

"He might not come until tomorrow morning or maybe tomorrow night. He didn't say when he would come," replied Mother.

Penny decided to cut out some new clothes for her paper dolls. She sat in the window seat where she could watch while she waited.

When she heard a car come down the street, she would glance up. Car after car went by.

At last Pete saw the light green car they were waiting for.

"He is here!" he shouted. "Daddy is here."

Pete and Penny both rushed out.

"We are glad you are here at last," Penny said. "We waited and watched and watched and waited."

At supper, Daddy told the family about his trip, and then he turned to Penny. "Just as you watched and waited for me to come, all of us are waiting for Jesus to come back."

"How do we know when He will come?" asked Penny.

"Jesus' friends asked the same question," replied Daddy. "I will read Jesus' answer from the Bible."

But of that day and hour knoweth no man, no, not the angels of heaven, but my Father only. But as the days of Noah were, so shall also the coming of the Son of man be. For as in the days that were before the flood they were eating and drinking, marrying and giving in marriage, until the day that Noah entered into the ark, and knew not until the flood came, and took them all away; so shall also the coming of the Son of man be. Then shall two be in the field; the one shall be taken, and the other left. Two women shall be grinding at the mill; the one shall be taken, and the other left. Watch therefore: for ye know not what hour your Lord doth come (Matthew 24:36-42).

"Will it really be like that?" asked Pete. "If two people are riding along in a car when Jesus comes in a cloud to get His own, will one go up and one stay in the car?"

"If one knows the Lord and the other does not, that is the way it will be."

"How long ago did Jesus promise to come back?" Penny asked, before she took another bite of pudding.

"Nearly two thousand years," replied Daddy.

Pete whistled. "That is a long time. Do you think He really will come?"

Daddy read another verse, " 'The Lord is not slack concerning his promise' (2 Peter 3:9)."

Then Daddy explained, "The Lord is not lazy about His promise. He promised to send His Son into the world the first time, and He came. He promised that Jesus would come back again, and He will."

Penny looked at Daddy. She looked at Pete, sitting across the table from her. Then she looked at Mother.

"I love you all," she said. "I am glad we are all Christians, so we can spend forever and ever in heaven with the Lord Jesus Christ, and with each other."

"There are lots of people who are not Christians,"

said Pete. "Let's ask God to help us live and give and do things to help some of them be saved."

So they did. Will you?

Moody Press, a ministry of the Moody Bible Institute, is designed for education, evangelization and edification. If we may assist you in knowing more about Christ and the Christian life, please write us without obligation to:
Moody Press, c/o MLM, Chicago, Illinois 60610.